DIGITAL REAL ESTATE

Practical Guide to Start, Launch or Invest in the Highly Profitable Global Digital Economy

IJIGBAN DANIEL OKETA

VOLUME ONE

All Rights Reserved.

Copyright © 2024 by Ijigban Daniel Oketa.

DIGITAL REAL ESTATE

ISBN: 9798329089462

No part of this publication may be reproduced, distributed, or transmitted in any form or by any means, including photocopying, recording, or other electronic or mechanical methods, without the prior written permission of the author and copyright holder, except in the case of brief quotations embodied in critical reviews and certain other noncommercial uses permitted by copyright law.

For permissions requests or inquiries, please contact.

+234 703-738-4814
oketadaniels@gmail.com

Contents

CHAPTER 1: PREFACE 4

CHAPTER 2: DIGITAL REAL ESTATE AND ECONOMY 7

CHAPTER 3: A WORLD OF DIGITAL REAL ESTATE PRODUCTS 20

CHAPTER 4: HOW TO GET STARTED WITH DIGITAL REAL ESTATE 30

CHAPTER 5: MONETIZING DIGITAL REAL ESTATE 38

CHAPTER 6: MANAGING AND GROWING YOUR DIGITAL REAL ESTATE 46

CHAPTER 7: CASE STUDIES AND SUCCESS STORIES 56

CHAPTER 8: LEGAL AND FINANCIAL CONSIDERATIONS 72

CHAPTER 8: TRENDS AND FUTURE OF DIGITAL REAL ESTATE 79

CHAPTER 10: TOOLS AND RESOURCES FOR DIGITAL REAL ESTATE 85

CHAPTER 11: COMMUNITY AND NETWORKING 91

CHAPTER 12: RECAP OF KEY THEMES 97

CHAPTER 13: CONCLUSION 101

Chapter 1: PREFACE

In the rapidly evolving landscape of the digital age, the concept of real estate has expanded beyond physical properties to encompass a diverse array of digital assets in the global digital economy.

Ideas are not just the new oil; to make the most of your ideas, you need to create digital real estate for your ideas.

You are a global citizen of the internet. You are already transacting in the digital economy, so long as you have used the internet directly or indirectly even if you only watched a video, used an email or own a mobile phone.

You should start a digital real estate business or invest in one and as many as possible. In today's world, the landscape of opportunity is defined by digital real estate.

Whether you are embarking on the journey of launching a digital real estate business or strategically investing in new or existing digital assets and business ventures, the potential for growth and profitability is undeniable.

Starting a digital real estate business allows you to carve out your niche in the virtual marketplace, leveraging your creativity, expertise, and vision to build valuable digital properties. From developing websites and mobile apps to creating engaging content and virtual experiences, the possibilities for innovation and profit are boundless.

On the other hand, investing in digital real estate presents a unique opportunity to capitalize on a proven business model or established assets with proven revenue streams.

In both scenarios, you can diversify your portfolio and tap into passive income streams to create financial wealth. The key lies in recognizing the transformative power of digital assets and seizing the opportunity to participate in the digital real estate market.

This book empowers you with a depth of Digital real estate and economy:

1. The difference between digital real estate and digital economy.

2. How to start, launch or invest in the highly profitable global real estate and digital economy.

3. Monetizing, managing and growing your digital real estate.

4. Case studies and success stories various investments in digital real estate.
5. Legal and financial considerations of digital real estate.
6. Trends and future of digital real estate.
7. Tools and resources for digital real estate.

Before it becomes too late for you, it is time to embrace the journey of digital real estate and unlock the potential for success or create a fortune in the digital age. I heard a story of a man who was offered an opportunity to buy into digital real estate but he rejected it. He later discovered the idea became worth $100billion in just 10 years. He regretted it.

I have advanced my knowledge of the internet as a computer instructor and analyst with knowledge of web and app development; I have built digital real estate products and currently developing my portfolio in Artificial Intelligence (AI) and the Internet Of Things (IOT). Having stayed in the digital economy for over twenty years, I am glad to be leading you on this journey.

Whether you are a budding entrepreneur or a savvy investor, the time to engage in digital real estate is now. Don't miss out on the chance to shape the future of online commerce, influence, and innovation.

Congratulations!
Yours Success Friend,
Ijigban Daniel Oketa

Chapter 2: DIGITAL REAL ESTATE AND ECONOMY

Digital Real Estate: Definition, Scope, and Types

Let's dive into the definition, importance, and evolution of digital real estate, setting the stage for exploring its various facets in detail.

Digital real estate refers to virtual properties that exist on the internet. These properties include websites, domain names, social media accounts, e-commerce stores, mobile apps, and even virtual spaces in online worlds.

Much like physical real estate, digital real estate can be bought, sold, leased, and developed. The value of digital real estate lies in its potential to generate income, attract traffic, and provide a platform for various online activities.

Why is Digital Real Estate Important?

The importance of digital real estate has surged in the past three decades, driven by the exponential growth of the internet and digital economy.

According to a report by eMarketer, global e-commerce sales reached $4.28 trillion in 2020 and are projected to hit $5.42 trillion by 2022. This trend underscores the significant economic opportunities in owning and managing digital assets.

Digital real estate offers several key benefits:

- **Income Generation**: Digital properties can generate passive income through advertising, affiliate marketing, product sales, and subscription models.

- **Scalability**: Unlike physical real estate, digital properties can reach a global audience without significant geographical limitations.

- **Low Overhead Costs**: Managing digital assets typically requires lower overhead costs compared to physical properties, making it a more accessible investment for many individuals and businesses.

- **Flexibility and Innovation**: Digital real estate allows for continuous innovation and adaptation, enabling owners to respond quickly to market changes and new opportunities.

Types of Digital Assets

1. **Websites and Blogs**: Websites are the most common form of digital real estate. They can serve various purposes, from personal blogs to business portals. Blogs, in particular, have gained popularity as platforms for sharing information and engaging with audiences. Monetization strategies for websites and blogs include display advertising, sponsored content, and affiliate marketing. According to Statista, the global digital advertising market reached $601.84 billion in 2023 and is estimated at $870.85 billion in 2027, reflecting the lucrative potential of well-trafficked websites.

2. **Domain Names**: Domain names are the digital equivalent of real-world addresses. Owning a valuable domain name can be highly profitable, as it is often the first point of contact for online users. Domain flipping, which involves buying and selling domain names for profit, has become a popular investment strategy. Premium domain names can sell for millions; for example, Voice.com was sold for $30 million in 2019.

3. **Social Media Accounts**: Social media platforms like Facebook, Instagram, Twitter, and TikTok offer significant opportunities for digital real estate investment. High-traffic social media accounts can be monetized through sponsored posts, influencer marketing, and direct product sales. According to Hootsuite, there were 4.48 billion social media users globally in 2021,

highlighting the vast audience accessible through these platforms.

4. **E-commerce Stores**: Online stores are another vital type of digital asset. Platforms like Shopify, WooCommerce, and Amazon enable entrepreneurs to set up and run e-commerce businesses with relative ease. The e-commerce market has seen unprecedented growth, with Statista projecting global retail e-commerce sales to reach $6.54 trillion by 2023. Successful e-commerce stores can be sold for a substantial profit, making them a valuable digital real estate investment.

5. **Mobile Apps**: Mobile apps represent a growing segment of digital real estate. With the increasing reliance on smartphones, apps have become essential tools for businesses and service providers. Monetization methods for mobile apps include in-app purchases, subscription services, and ad revenue. According to App Annie, global consumer spending on mobile apps reached $143 billion in 2020, indicating a thriving market for app developers and investors.

6. **Digital Real Estate in Virtual Worlds**: Virtual worlds like Decentraland and The Sandbox offer innovative digital real estate opportunities. Users can buy, sell, and develop virtual land, creating immersive experiences and generating income through activities like virtual events and advertising. The market for virtual real estate is

expanding rapidly, with CNBC reporting that virtual land sales topped $500 million in 2021.

Digital real estate represents a dynamic and profitable frontier in the digital economy. Understanding its definition, importance, and types can help individuals and businesses capitalize on the numerous opportunities it offers. As the internet continues to evolve, the scope of digital real estate will likely expand, making it an increasingly vital asset in the modern economy.

The Tale of Two Entrepreneurs:

Navigating Digital Real Estate and the Digital Economy

Let's say you are Emma or Jake in this fictional story. Once upon a time in the thriving town of Technopolis, two friends, Emma and Jake, embarked on a journey into the vast and intriguing world of the internet. Emma, a creative visionary with a knack for identifying hidden gems, and Jake, a tech-savvy strategist with a passion for innovation, set out to explore the burgeoning opportunities of the digital age.

Emma's Venture into Digital Real Estate

Emma was always fascinated by the idea of owning something valuable. When she learned about digital real estate, her eyes lit up with excitement. She saw potential in owning digital properties just as one might own prime physical real estate in the heart of a bustling city.

Emma started small, purchasing a domain name that sounded catchy and memorable. She built a blog around her love for sustainable living, creating engaging content that drew a steady stream of visitors. Through diligent SEO practices and consistent content creation, her blog began to rank high on search engines. She monetized it through affiliate marketing, collaborating with eco-friendly brands, and soon, her website was generating a comfortable income.

Not stopping there, Emma ventured into buying and selling domain names. She researched trends, identified valuable domains, and flipped them for profit. Each successful sale was a step closer to her dream of becoming a digital real estate mogul. She expanded her portfolio to include social media accounts, e-commerce stores, and even virtual properties in emerging virtual worlds.

Jake's Exploration of the Digital Economy

Meanwhile, Jake was captivated by the broader digital economy. He saw the internet not just as a marketplace, but as a vast ecosystem where innovation and technology could revolutionize traditional industries. Jake decided to launch an online marketplace that connected local artisans with global customers. His platform utilized advanced algorithms to match buyers with sellers, offering a seamless shopping experience.

Jake also delved into the world of FinTech, developing an app that simplified online payments and brought banking services to underserved communities. His ventures extended to digital marketing services, where he helped other businesses navigate the complexities of online advertising and social media strategies. He even invested in a cloud computing startup, understanding the critical role digital infrastructure played in the digital economy.

The Intersection of Emma and Jake's Worlds

Emma and Jake often shared their experiences over coffee. Emma's tales of flipping domain names and monetizing websites fascinated Jake, while Jake's stories of revolutionizing industries through digital services inspired Emma. They realized that while they were operating in different spheres—Emma in digital real estate and Jake in the digital economy—there was significant overlap in their endeavors.

Emma's digital properties benefited from the broader digital economy that Jake was helping to build. Jake's platforms and services relied on the digital assets that Emma and others like her were developing and managing. Together, they painted a comprehensive picture of how the internet was transforming every aspect of life and business.

Lessons and Legacy

Their journeys taught them valuable lessons about the digital age. Emma learned the importance of continuous learning and adaptation in managing digital assets. Jake discovered the power of collaboration and innovation in driving economic growth. Both understood that the key to success lay in recognizing and seizing the opportunities that the digital world offered.

Their combined experiences highlighted the distinction and interplay between digital real estate and the digital economy. Digital real estate, with its focus on owning and monetizing specific online properties, provided a foundation. The digital economy, with its broad range of economic activities facilitated by digital technologies, offered endless possibilities for innovation and expansion.

As Technopolis grew into a hub of digital innovation, Emma and Jake became mentors to aspiring digital entrepreneurs. They shared their stories, imparting wisdom and inspiring others to explore the boundless opportunities of the digital landscape. And thus, in the heart of Technopolis, the legacy of Emma and Jake lived on, shaping the future of the digital age, one innovative idea at a time.

History and Evolution of Digital Real Estate

Digital real estate has evolved remarkably from its inception in the early days of the internet to its current state as a multifaceted and lucrative domain. This chapter traces the historical development of digital real estate, beginning with the advent of the internet and the emergence of the first websites. It explores the rise of digital properties, highlighting key milestones such as the expansion of e-commerce, the social media revolution, and the growth of mobile and app ecosystems. Additionally, we delve into the recent advancements in cloud computing, virtual realities, and blockchain technologies, which have further transformed the digital real estate landscape. By examining this evolution, we gain valuable insights into the past, present, and future of digital property ownership and investment.

Early Days of the Internet

The Advent of the Internet

The concept of the Internet began as an experiment in communication and data sharing. In the 1960s, the U.S. Department of Defense initiated the ARPANET project, aimed at creating a robust, fault-tolerant communication network. This initial network connected a handful of academic and research institutions, setting the foundation for what would become the Internet.

By the early 1980s, advancements in computer networking and protocols such as TCP/IP allowed for a more extensive and interconnected network. This period saw the birth of domains and the Domain Name System (DNS), which provided a human-readable way to access the web. Websites like Symbolics.com, registered in 1985, became the first digital real estate, marking the dawn of an era where web addresses held intrinsic value.

The First Websites and Early Commerce

In the mid-1990s, the Internet transitioned from a primarily academic and government tool to a commercial and public medium. The introduction of the World Wide Web by Tim Berners-Lee in 1991 revolutionized digital communication, allowing for a graphical interface and hyperlinks, which made navigating the Internet more accessible and intuitive.

Websites like Yahoo (1994) and Amazon (1995) emerged as pioneers in digital real estate. Yahoo started as a simple directory but quickly grew into a vast portal, demonstrating the potential of digital property to attract vast audiences. Amazon, initially an online bookstore, showcased the commercial possibilities of the Internet, foreshadowing the rise of e-commerce.

During this time, domain names became increasingly valuable as they served as the primary addresses of the burgeoning web. The registration of generic domain names such as Business.com, which was sold for $7.5 million in 1999, highlighted the growing recognition of digital real estate's worth.

The Rise of Digital Properties

Expansion of E-Commerce and Digital Services

The late 1990s and early 2000s saw an explosion in the number of websites and the services they offered. E-commerce platforms like eBay (1995) and PayPal (1998) facilitated online transactions, further integrating the Internet into daily commercial activities. These platforms not only transformed shopping habits but also demonstrated the immense potential of digital real estate as a marketplace.

Search engines like Google (1998) revolutionized how users navigate the web, making it easier to find information and services. Google's AdWords program, launched in 2000, allowed businesses to purchase digital advertising space, introducing a new form of digital real estate monetization. This shift marked the beginning of the Internet as a lucrative advertising platform, where website traffic translated directly into revenue. 2024, the Google search entire is worth over $2trillion bringing in over $500 billion in revenue.

The Social Media Revolution

The mid-2000s brought the rise of social media, which fundamentally altered the landscape of digital real estate. Platforms like Facebook (2004), YouTube (2005), and Twitter (2006) became central hubs of online interaction and content sharing. These sites turned user-generated content into valuable digital real estate, where engagement and community-building became key drivers of value.

Facebook's advertising model, based on user data and targeted ads, demonstrated a new level of sophistication in monetizing digital real estate. Similarly, YouTube's Partner Program, launched in 2007, allowed content creators to earn revenue, highlighting the potential of user-generated digital properties.

The Mobile and App Ecosystem

The introduction of smartphones, particularly with the launch of the iPhone in 2007, expanded digital real estate into the mobile domain. App stores like Apple's App Store (2008) and Google Play (2008) created new opportunities for digital property development. Apps became valuable digital real estate, with popular applications attracting millions of users and generating significant revenue.

Mobile-responsive websites and the growth of mobile commerce further emphasized the importance of digital real estate optimization. Businesses needed to ensure their digital properties were accessible and user-friendly on mobile devices to capitalize on this growing market segment.

The Cloud and Virtual Realities

The 2010s saw advancements in cloud computing and virtual realities, which expanded the concept of digital real estate. Cloud services like Amazon Web Services (AWS) and Microsoft Azure provided the infrastructure for scalable digital properties, allowing businesses to host complex applications and services without significant upfront investment.

Virtual and augmented reality technologies, exemplified by platforms like Second Life and more recently, the Metaverse, introduced entirely new dimensions of digital real estate. These virtual environments allowed users to create, buy, and sell virtual properties, blending the boundaries between the digital and physical worlds.

The Blockchain and NFT Era

The late 2010s and early 2020s introduced blockchain technology and non-fungible tokens (NFTs), revolutionizing the concept of ownership and value in digital real estate. Blockchain ensured secure, transparent transactions, while NFTs allowed for unique digital assets that could be bought, sold, and traded.

Platforms like Decentraland and Cryptovoxels emerged, offering virtual worlds where users could purchase and develop land using cryptocurrencies. These digital real estate markets functioned similarly to physical real estate, with location, development potential, and demand influencing value.

The Future of Digital Real Estate

As technology continues to evolve, the future of digital real estate looks promising. The integration of artificial intelligence, enhanced virtual realities, and advanced blockchain applications will likely drive further innovation. Digital properties will become increasingly sophisticated, with greater interactivity and customization.

In this evolving landscape, understanding the history and development of digital real estate provides valuable insights into its future potential. From the early days of simple web directories to the complex virtual worlds and blockchain-based assets of today, digital real estate has proven to be a dynamic and integral part of the modern economy.

Chapter 3: A WORLD OF DIGITAL REAL ESTATE PRODUCTS

The realm of digital real estate is vast and varied, encompassing a wide range of virtual properties that offer unique opportunities for investment and growth.

This chapter explores the different types of digital real estate, from traditional websites and blogs to the dynamic world of social media accounts, e-commerce stores, and mobile apps.

We'll also delve into the emerging frontier of virtual and augmented reality properties, as well as the intriguing possibilities presented by blockchain and non-fungible tokens (NFTs).

By understanding the various forms of digital real estate, their benefits, and strategies for acquisition and monetization, you can effectively navigate this ever-evolving landscape and capitalize on its immense potential.

Websites and Blogs

Benefits of Owning a Website

Owning a website offers numerous advantages for individuals and businesses. Firstly, it provides a platform for establishing an online presence and showcasing products, services, or personal content.

Websites serve as digital storefronts, accessible 24/7, allowing businesses to reach a global audience beyond geographical constraints.

A website also enables control over brand identity and messaging. Owners can customize the design, content, and functionality to align with their vision and goals. This level of control is crucial for maintaining brand consistency and fostering customer trust.

Additionally, websites offer opportunities for data collection and analysis. Tools like Google Analytics allow owners to track visitor behavior, measure engagement, and gain insights into customer preferences. This data-driven approach facilitates informed decision-making and enhances marketing strategies.

Monetization Strategies for Websites and Blogs

Monetizing a website or blog can be achieved through various strategies:

1. **Advertising**: Displaying ads through networks like Google AdSense can generate revenue based

on impressions or clicks. Sponsored content and affiliate marketing are other advertising avenues.

2. **E-commerce**: Integrating an online store allows for selling products or services directly to visitors. This can range from physical goods to digital products like e-books or software.

3. **Subscription Models**: Offering premium content or services behind a paywall can attract subscribers. Membership sites, online courses, and exclusive content are popular subscription-based models.

4. **Sponsored Posts**: Collaborating with brands to create sponsored content provides an income stream while adding value to the audience.

5. **Donations and Crowdfunding**: Platforms like Patreon enable content creators to receive financial support from their audience.

Domain Names

How to Choose Valuable Domain Names

Choosing a valuable domain name involves several key considerations:

1. **Relevance**: The domain should reflect the website's content or business. Keywords related to the industry can enhance search engine optimization (SEO).

2. **Simplicity**: A short, memorable, and easy-to-spell domain is more likely to attract visitors and be shared.

3. **Brandability**: Unique and brandable domains stand out and are easier to market. Avoid generic names that may be confused with other sites.

4. **Extensions**: While .com is the most recognized extension, others like .net, .org, or industry-specific extensions (e.g., .tech, .shop) can also be valuable.

5. **Avoiding Legal Issues**: Ensure the domain does not infringe on trademarks or copyrights to avoid legal complications.

Domain Flipping: Buying and Selling Domains

Domain flipping involves purchasing domains at a low price and selling them for a profit. Successful domain flipping requires:

1. **Research**: Identify domains with potential value, considering factors like keyword relevance, market trends, and existing demand.

2. **Timing**: Purchase domains when they are undervalued and sell when there is increased interest or demand.

3. **Marketing**: Effectively market the domain to potential buyers through platforms like GoDaddy Auctions, Sedo, or Flippa.

4. **Negotiation**: Skillful negotiation can maximize the sale price of a domain.

Social Media Accounts

Leveraging Social Media for Business

Social media accounts are valuable digital real estate for businesses. They provide platforms for marketing, customer engagement, and brand building. Key benefits include:

1. **Reach and Engagement**: Social media allows businesses to reach a vast audience and engage with customers in real-time.

2. **Targeted Advertising**: Platforms like Facebook, Instagram, and LinkedIn offer sophisticated targeting options, enabling businesses to reach specific demographics.

3. **Brand Loyalty**: Consistent, engaging content fosters a loyal community and enhances brand perception.

4. **Customer Feedback**: Social media serves as a channel for direct customer feedback, helping businesses improve their products and services.

Buying and Selling Social Media Accounts

Buying and selling social media accounts involves the following:

1. **Valuation**: Assess the value of an account based on factors like follower count, engagement rate, niche relevance, and monetization potential.

2. **Marketplaces**: Use platforms like Fameswap or Social Tradia to buy or sell accounts securely.

3. **Compliance**: Ensure transactions comply with the terms of service of the social media platform to avoid account suspension.

E-commerce Stores

Building and Selling Online Stores

Building an e-commerce store involves:

1. **Platform Selection**: Choose a platform like Shopify, WooCommerce, or BigCommerce based on needs and budget.

2. **Product Selection**: Identify and source products that meet market demand.

3. **Website Design**: Create an attractive, user-friendly website to enhance the shopping experience.

4. **Marketing**: Utilize SEO, social media marketing, and email campaigns to drive traffic and sales.

Selling an e-commerce store requires:

1. **Valuation**: Determine the store's value based on revenue, profit margins, traffic, and growth potential.

2. **Marketplaces**: Use platforms like Flippa or Empire Flippers to list and sell the store.

3. **Due Diligence**: Provide comprehensive data and insights to potential buyers to facilitate a smooth transaction.

Marketplaces for Buying E-commerce Businesses

Marketplaces like Flippa, Empire Flippers, and FE International offer platforms to buy and sell e-commerce businesses. These marketplaces provide:

1. **Listings**: Detailed listings with financial data, traffic statistics, and growth opportunities.

2. **Verification**: Verification services to ensure the legitimacy of the business.

3. **Support**: Assistance with negotiations, legal documentation, and transfer processes.

Mobile Apps

Development and Monetization of Mobile Apps

Developing a mobile app involves:

1. **Conceptualization**: Identify a unique value proposition and target audience.

2. **Design and Development**: Create a user-friendly design and develop the app using platforms like iOS or Android.

3. **Testing**: Conduct thorough testing to ensure functionality and usability.

Monetizing a mobile app can be achieved through:

1. **In-App Advertising**: Display ads within the app using networks like AdMob.

2. **In-App Purchases**: Offer additional features, content, or virtual goods for purchase.

3. **Subscription Models**: Provide premium content or services on a subscription basis.

4. **Paid Apps**: Charge a one-time fee for app download.

Buying and Selling Mobile Apps

Buying and selling mobile apps involves:

1. **Valuation**: Assess the app's value based on downloads, user engagement, revenue, and growth potential.

2. **Marketplaces**: Use platforms like Flippa or Apptopia to list and sell apps.

3. **Due Diligence**: Ensure comprehensive data is available for potential buyers, including source code, user metrics, and financial performance.

Digital Real Estate in Virtual Worlds

Virtual Reality and Augmented Reality Properties

Virtual reality (VR) and augmented reality (AR) properties represent a new frontier in digital real estate. These properties exist within virtual environments where users can interact with digital spaces and assets.

1. **VR Platforms**: Platforms like Decentraland, The Sandbox, and VRChat allow users to buy, sell, and develop virtual land.

2. **AR Applications**: AR enhances real-world environments with digital overlays, offering opportunities for innovative marketing and interactive experiences.

Investing in Virtual Real Estate

Investing in virtual real estate involves:

1. **Research**: Understand the platform, its user base, and potential for growth.

2. **Acquisition**: Purchase virtual land or assets using cryptocurrencies or platform-specific tokens.

3. **Development**: Enhance the value of virtual properties by creating engaging and interactive environments.

4. **Monetization**: Generate revenue through virtual events, advertising, or selling developed properties.

In conclusion, the diverse types of digital real estate offer a myriad of opportunities for investment, development, and monetization.

From traditional websites and blogs to emerging virtual and augmented realities, each type presents unique challenges and rewards, underscoring the dynamic and evolving nature of digital property.

Chapter 4: HOW TO GET STARTED WITH DIGITAL REAL ESTATE

In today's digital age, owning virtual properties has become as valuable as owning physical real estate. From websites and blogs to domain names, social media accounts, e-commerce stores, mobile apps, and even virtual reality properties, digital real estate offers a plethora of opportunities for entrepreneurs and investors alike.

This chapter delves into the essential steps for getting started in the world of digital real estate. We will explore how to identify a niche that aligns with both market demand and personal passion, the process of acquiring digital assets, and the fundamentals of building and optimizing your digital property.

Whether you're looking to generate passive income, expand your business, or invest in the digital frontier, this guide will provide the insights and strategies you need to embark on a successful digital real estate journey.

Identifying Your Niche

Research and Market Analysis

The first step in embarking on your digital real estate journey is identifying a niche that aligns with market demand and your interests. Conducting thorough research and market analysis is crucial to this process. Here's how to get started:

1. **Industry Trends**: Stay informed about current trends in various industries by following news, subscribing to industry publications, and attending webinars and conferences. Platforms like Google Trends, Statista, and industry reports can provide valuable insights into what's trending.

2. **Competitor Analysis**: Identify potential competitors within your chosen niche. Analyze their websites, content, marketing strategies, and customer engagement. Tools like SEMrush, Ahrefs, and SimilarWeb can help you understand competitor performance and traffic sources.

3. **Audience Research**: Understand the demographics, preferences, and behaviors of your target audience. Use tools like Google Analytics, social media insights, and surveys to

gather data. Knowing your audience will help tailor your digital property to meet their needs.

4. **Keyword Research**: Identify high-volume, low-competition keywords related to your niche. This will inform your content strategy and improve your website's search engine visibility. Tools like Google Keyword Planner, Ubersuggest, and Moz can assist in this process.

Finding Your Passion and Expertise

Choosing a niche that aligns with your passion and expertise can significantly impact your success and sustainability. Here's how to find your niche:

1. **Self-Assessment**: Reflect on your interests, hobbies, and professional background. What topics excite you? What skills and knowledge do you possess? Aligning your niche with your passion ensures long-term commitment and enthusiasm.

2. **Identify Problems and Solutions**: Consider problems or pain points within your areas of interest. Can you offer solutions or valuable insights? Niche markets often thrive when they address specific challenges or unmet needs.

3. **Evaluate Profitability**: While passion is essential, profitability is equally important. Assess the revenue potential of your chosen niche. Look for niches with demand, but avoid

oversaturated markets unless you can offer a unique angle.

Acquiring Digital Real Estate

Where to Buy Digital Assets

Once you've identified your niche, the next step is acquiring digital real estate. There are various platforms and marketplaces where you can buy digital assets, including:

1. **Domain Marketplaces**: Platforms like GoDaddy Auctions, Sedo, and Namecheap allow you to purchase domain names. Look for domains that are relevant, memorable, and have good SEO potential.

2. **Website Marketplaces**: Websites like Flippa, Empire Flippers, and FE International specialize in buying and selling established websites and online businesses. These platforms provide detailed listings with performance metrics, making it easier to find a suitable investment.

3. **App Marketplaces**: If you're interested in mobile apps, platforms like Apptopia and Flippa offer opportunities to buy existing apps with established user bases and revenue streams.

4. **Virtual Real Estate Platforms**: For those interested in virtual worlds and VR/AR properties, platforms like Decentraland, The Sandbox, and Cryptovoxels facilitate the

purchase of virtual land and assets using cryptocurrencies.

Valuation and Due Diligence

Before making a purchase, conducting thorough valuation and due diligence is critical to ensure you're making a sound investment. Here's how to proceed:

1. **Financial Performance**: Review the financial records of the digital asset, including revenue, expenses, and profit margins. Ensure the numbers are accurate and sustainable.

2. **Traffic and Engagement**: Analyze traffic data to understand the asset's performance and potential for growth. Look for consistent traffic patterns, high engagement rates, and low bounce rates.

3. **SEO and Rankings**: Evaluate the asset's search engine rankings and keyword performance. Ensure there are no penalties or black-hat SEO practices that could harm future growth.

4. **Technical and Security Audits**: Conduct a technical audit to identify any issues with website performance, security vulnerabilities, or outdated technology. Tools like Google PageSpeed Insights, GTmetrix, and Sucuri can assist in this process.

5. **Legal Considerations**: Verify ownership and ensure there are no legal disputes or copyright infringements associated with the digital asset.

Review contracts and seek legal advice if necessary.

Building Your Digital Property

Website Development Basics

Building a website is a foundational step in establishing your digital real estate. Here are the basics of website development:

1. **Choosing a Platform**: Select a content management system (CMS) that suits your needs. WordPress, Wix, and Shopify are popular choices for different types of websites. WordPress is highly customizable and ideal for blogs and content-rich sites, while Shopify is tailored for e-commerce.

2. **Domain and Hosting**: Purchase a domain name and choose a reliable hosting provider. Hosting services like Bluehost, SiteGround, and WP Engine offer various plans based on your website's requirements.

3. **Design and User Experience**: Focus on creating an intuitive and visually appealing design. Use themes and templates to streamline the process, but ensure your site is unique and reflective of your brand. Prioritize user experience by making navigation easy and ensuring the site is mobile-responsive.

4. **Content Management**: Organize your content effectively using categories and tags. Create a content calendar to plan and publish regular updates, ensuring your site remains fresh and engaging.

SEO and Content Marketing

Optimizing your website for search engines and implementing effective content marketing strategies are crucial for driving traffic and achieving success. Here's how to get started:

1. **On-Page SEO**: Optimize individual pages by using relevant keywords in titles, headings, meta descriptions, and content. Ensure your site's structure is clean, with proper use of header tags (H1, H2, H3, etc.) and internal linking.

2. **Technical SEO**: Improve your site's technical performance by enhancing page load speed, ensuring mobile-friendliness, and implementing secure HTTPS protocols. Regularly check for crawl errors and fix broken links.

3. **Quality Content**: Create high-quality, valuable content that addresses your audience's needs and interests. Use a mix of blog posts, articles, videos, and infographics to keep your content diverse and engaging.

4. **Content Marketing**: Promote your content through various channels, including social media, email marketing, and guest blogging. Building

backlinks from reputable sites can also boost your SEO efforts and drive organic traffic.

5. **Analytics and Adjustments**: Use tools like Google Analytics and Google Search Console to monitor your site's performance. Analyze traffic patterns, user behavior, and conversion rates to identify areas for improvement and adjust your strategies accordingly.

The lists of services and products or channels mentioned are endless.

By following these steps, you can effectively enter the world of digital real estate, acquiring valuable assets, building engaging properties, and driving success through strategic marketing and optimization efforts.

The digital landscape offers boundless opportunities, and with careful planning and execution, you can establish a thriving presence in this dynamic field.

Chapter 5: MONETIZING DIGITAL REAL ESTATE

The potential to generate income from digital real estate is vast and varied. Whether you own a blog, a website, a social media account, or an e-commerce store, there are numerous strategies you can employ to monetize your digital property.

This chapter delves into four primary methods: affiliate marketing, advertising, selling digital products, and subscription models. Each method offers unique opportunities and challenges, which we will explore in detail.

Affiliate Marketing

Choosing Affiliate Programs

Affiliate marketing is a popular way to monetize digital real estate by promoting other companies' products or services and earning a commission on any sales generated through your referral links. The success of your affiliate marketing efforts largely depends on choosing the right affiliate programs.

1. **Relevance**: Select programs that align with your niche and audience. Promoting relevant products ensures higher engagement and conversion rates. For instance, a tech blog would benefit more from promoting gadgets or software rather than unrelated products like fashion accessories.

2. **Commission Rates**: Compare the commission rates offered by different programs. While typical rates range from 5% to 20%, some programs offer higher commissions for high-ticket items or recurring payments for subscription services.

3. **Cookie Duration**: Cookie duration refers to the length of time a referral link remains active. Longer cookie durations (30 days or more) increase the likelihood of earning a commission.

4. **Reputation**: Partner with reputable companies that offer quality products and reliable payments. Research reviews and testimonials to ensure you're affiliating with trustworthy brands.

Strategies for Effective Affiliate Marketing

1. **Content Quality**: Create high-quality, informative content that naturally incorporates affiliate links. Product reviews, comparison articles, and how-to guides are effective formats for promoting affiliate products.

2. **SEO Optimization**: Optimize your content for search engines to increase organic traffic. Use relevant keywords, meta descriptions, and quality backlinks to improve your site's visibility.

3. **Email Marketing**: Build an email list and send targeted newsletters featuring affiliate products. Personalized recommendations can significantly boost conversion rates.

4. **Social Media**: Leverage social media platforms to promote affiliate products. Engage with your audience through posts, stories, and live sessions to build trust and drive traffic to your affiliate links.

Advertising

Google AdSense and Other Ad Networks

Advertising is a straightforward way to monetize digital real estate by displaying ads on your website or blog. Google AdSense is one of the most popular ad networks, but there are many other options available.

1. **Google AdSense**: AdSense allows you to display targeted ads on your site and earn revenue based on clicks (CPC) or impressions (CPM). Setting up AdSense is relatively easy, and the platform handles ad placement and optimization.

2. **Other Ad Networks**: Consider alternative ad networks like Media.net, AdThrive, and Ezoic, which may offer competitive rates and additional

features. These networks often cater to specific niches, which can result in better-targeted ads and higher earnings.

3. **Statistics**: As of 2022, the average CPM for Google AdSense ranges from $1 to $3, while premium networks like AdThrive can offer CPM rates between $15 and $25, depending on the niche and audience.

Direct Advertising Sales

Direct advertising involves selling ad space on your website or blog directly to businesses. This approach allows you to negotiate rates and establish long-term partnerships.

1. **Rate Cards**: Develop a rate card that outlines your advertising options, including banner ads, sponsored posts, and newsletter placements. Clearly state your pricing, traffic metrics, and audience demographics.

2. **Outreach**: Proactively reach out to potential advertisers within your niche. Personalized pitches that highlight the benefits of advertising on your site can attract more interest.

3. **Contracts**: Establish clear contracts that define the terms of the advertising agreement, including payment schedules, ad placements, and performance metrics.

Selling Digital Products

Creating and Selling E-books, Courses, and Software

Selling digital products is a highly profitable way to monetize digital real estate. Digital products such as e-books, online courses, and software have low production costs and can generate passive income.

1. **E-books**: Write e-books on topics relevant to your audience. Use platforms like Amazon Kindle Direct Publishing (KDP) or sell directly through your website using tools like Gumroad or Payhip.

2. **Online Courses**: Create comprehensive online courses using platforms like Teachable, Udemy, or Kajabi. Courses can include video lectures, downloadable resources, and interactive quizzes.

3. **Software**: Develop and sell software solutions that address specific needs within your niche. Offer free trials or freemium models to attract users and upsell premium features.

4. **Statistics**: The global e-learning market is projected to reach $375 billion by 2026, highlighting the lucrative potential of online courses. Similarly, the e-book market is expected to grow at a CAGR of 3.7% from 2021 to 2028.

Digital Product Marketplaces

1. **Marketplaces**: List your digital products on marketplaces like Etsy (for digital art and templates), AppSumo (for software), or Amazon (for e-books). These platforms provide access to a large customer base and additional marketing support.

2. **Promotion**: Utilize social media, email marketing, and SEO to drive traffic to your product listings. Collaborate with influencers or affiliates to expand your reach.

Subscription Models

Membership Sites

Membership sites offer exclusive content, products, or services to subscribers for a recurring fee. This model provides a steady income stream and fosters a loyal community.

1. **Content**: Offer valuable and unique content that justifies the subscription fee. This can include premium articles, videos, webinars, or access to a private community.

2. **Pricing Tiers**: Create multiple pricing tiers to cater to different customer segments. Offer additional perks for higher-tier memberships to encourage upgrades.

3. **Platform**: Use platforms like MemberPress, Patreon, or Substack to manage memberships and deliver content.

4. **Statistics**: Membership sites can be highly profitable, with successful creators on Patreon earning over $1,000 per month from dedicated subscribers.

Premium Content and Services

Offering premium content and services is another effective subscription model. This can include advanced tutorials, consulting services, or access to exclusive tools and resources.

1. **Premium Blogs**: Create a section of your blog that offers in-depth articles, industry reports, or expert interviews accessible only to subscribers.

2. **Consulting**: Offer one-on-one consulting services or group coaching sessions for a monthly fee. This model works well for niches like business, health, and personal development.

3. **Tools and Resources**: Develop and offer access to premium tools, templates, or resources that provide significant value to your audience.

In conclusion, monetizing digital real estate involves a diverse range of strategies, each with its unique advantages and potential for revenue generation.

By understanding and implementing these methods—affiliate marketing, advertising, selling digital products, and subscription models—you can effectively leverage your digital property to create sustainable and lucrative income streams.

Chapter 6: MANAGING AND GROWING YOUR DIGITAL REAL ESTATE

Once you've established your digital real estate, the next step is to manage and grow it effectively. This chapter will guide you through the essential strategies for content creation, traffic generation, and optimization. By focusing on these key areas, you can maximize your digital property's potential and ensure long-term success.

Content Creation and Strategy

Blogging and Video Content

Content is the cornerstone of any successful digital property. High-quality content not only attracts visitors but also keeps them engaged and encourages repeat visits. Here's how to approach blogging and video content creation:

1. **Blogging**: Blogs are a powerful tool for sharing information, building authority, and driving traffic. To create compelling blog content:

    o **Identify Audience Needs**: Understand what your audience is searching for and create content that addresses their questions and problems.

    o **Use Keywords**: Incorporate relevant keywords to improve search engine visibility. Tools like Google Keyword Planner and Ahrefs can help you find popular keywords in your niche.

    o **Engaging Titles**: Craft catchy and descriptive titles that entice readers to click. According to HubSpot, headlines with numbers or questions tend to perform better.

    o **Quality and Consistency**: Focus on providing value through well-researched and well-written posts. Aim for a consistent posting schedule, as blogs that post frequently receive 55% more visitors.

2. **Video Content**: Videos are highly engaging and can significantly boost your digital presence. For effective video content:

    o **Identify Your Platform**: Choose the right platform (YouTube, Vimeo, TikTok, etc.) based on where your audience spends their time.

- **Content Types**: Create a mix of content types, such as tutorials, product reviews, vlogs, and interviews. According to Wyzowl, 84% of people say that they've been convinced to buy a product or service by watching a brand's video.

- **SEO for Videos**: Optimize your video titles, descriptions, and tags with relevant keywords. This helps improve visibility in search results.

- **Consistency and Quality**: Maintain a regular posting schedule and invest in good equipment for high-quality production. High-definition videos are preferred by 68% of users.

Content Planning and Scheduling

Effective content planning and scheduling are crucial for maintaining a steady flow of fresh and relevant content. Here's how to manage your content strategy:

1. **Content Calendar**: Develop a content calendar to plan your posts in advance. This helps ensure a consistent posting schedule and allows you to plan around key dates and events.

- o **Tools**: Use tools like Trello, Asana, or Google Calendar to organize your content schedule.

- o **Variety**: Include a mix of content types (blogs, videos, infographics) and topics to keep your audience engaged.

2. **Editorial Guidelines**: Establish editorial guidelines to maintain a consistent voice and quality across all content. This includes tone, style, and formatting preferences.

3. **Repurposing Content**: Maximize your content's reach by repurposing it into different formats. For example, turn a blog post into a video, infographic, or podcast.

Traffic Generation

SEO Best Practices

Search Engine Optimization (SEO) is essential for increasing your digital property's visibility and driving organic traffic. Here's how to implement effective SEO strategies:

1. **On-Page SEO**: Optimize individual pages on your website to rank higher and earn more relevant traffic.

- **Keyword Optimization**: Use targeted keywords in your titles, headers, meta descriptions, and content.

- **Content Quality**: Create high-quality, informative content that answers users' queries. Longer content (over 1,500 words) tends to rank better.

- **Internal Linking**: Use internal links to help search engines understand the structure of your site and improve navigation.

2. **Off-Page SEO**: Enhance your site's authority through external methods.

    - **Backlinks**: Earn backlinks from reputable websites. According to Backlinko, the number of domains linking to a page is the most important ranking factor.

    - **Social Signals**: Engage with your audience on social media to increase your content's visibility and drive traffic.

3. **Technical SEO**: Ensure your website is technically sound and accessible to search engines.

    - **Site Speed**: Improve your site's loading speed, as faster sites rank better. Google reports that a one-second delay in mobile load times can impact mobile conversions by up to 20%.

- **Mobile Optimization**: Ensure your site is mobile-friendly, as mobile searches account for over half of all online searches.

Social Media Marketing

Social media platforms are powerful tools for driving traffic and building an online presence. Here's how to leverage social media for growth:

1. **Platform Selection**: Choose the right platforms based on your target audience. For example, Instagram and TikTok are popular with younger demographics, while Facebook and LinkedIn cater to older and professional audiences.

2. **Content Strategy**: Create engaging and shareable content tailored to each platform. Use a mix of posts, stories, and live sessions to engage with your audience.

3. **Community Engagement**: Actively engage with your audience by responding to comments, participating in discussions, and running contests or polls. This helps build a loyal community.

4. **Advertising**: Use social media ads to reach a broader audience. Platforms like Facebook and Instagram offer advanced targeting options to reach specific demographics.

Email Marketing

Email marketing is a highly effective way to nurture relationships and drive repeat traffic. Here's how to use email marketing effectively:

1. **Build Your List**: Collect email addresses through sign-up forms, lead magnets (e.g., free e-books, webinars), and content upgrades.

2. **Segmentation**: Segment your email list based on user behavior, demographics, and preferences. This allows you to send personalized and relevant content.

3. **Engaging Content**: Create compelling email content with clear calls to action (CTAs). Use a mix of newsletters, promotional emails, and personalized messages.

4. **Automation**: Use email marketing platforms like Mailchimp, ConvertKit, or ActiveCampaign to automate your email campaigns. Automation can help you send timely and relevant messages, such as welcome emails and follow-up sequences.

Analytics and Optimization

Using Google Analytics

Google Analytics is a powerful tool for tracking and analyzing your website's performance. Here's how to use it effectively:

1. **Set Up Goals**: Define and set up goals to track important actions on your site, such as form submissions, downloads, and purchases.

2. **Monitor Key Metrics**: Track key performance indicators (KPIs) such as traffic sources, bounce rates, average session duration, and conversion rates. This helps you understand your audience's behavior and identify areas for improvement.

3. **Audience Insights**: Use audience reports to gain insights into your visitors' demographics, interests, and geographic locations. This information can inform your content and marketing strategies.

4. **Behavior Flow**: Analyze the behavior flow to see how users navigate your site. Identify drop-off points and optimize those pages to improve user experience.

A/B Testing and Conversion Rate Optimization

A/B testing and conversion rate optimization (CRO) are essential for improving your site's performance and increasing conversions. Here's how to implement these strategies:

1. **A/B Testing**: Conduct A/B tests to compare different versions of a webpage or element (e.g., headlines, CTAs, images) to see which performs better.

- **Tools**: Use tools like Optimizely, VWO, or Google Optimize to run A/B tests.

- **Analyze Results**: Review the test results and implement the winning variation to improve performance.

2. **Conversion Rate Optimization**: Continuously optimize your site to increase the percentage of visitors who take desired actions.

    - **User Feedback**: Collect feedback from users through surveys or usability tests to identify pain points.

    - **Landing Pages**: Create focused and compelling landing pages with clear CTAs. According to Unbounce, the average conversion rate for landing pages is 9.7%.

3. **Heatmaps and Session Recordings**: Use tools like Hotjar or Crazy Egg to visualize user behavior through heatmaps and session recordings. This helps you understand how users interact with your site and identify areas for improvement.

In conclusion, managing and growing your digital real estate involves a combination of content creation, traffic generation, and optimization strategies. By focusing on high-quality content, leveraging various marketing channels, and continually analyzing and improving your performance, you can maximize the potential of your digital property and achieve long-term success.

Chapter 7: CASE STUDIES AND SUCCESS STORIES

In the dynamic world of digital real estate, countless individuals have transformed their visions into thriving businesses and lucrative investments.

This chapter delves into the inspiring stories of digital real estate entrepreneurs from around the globe, highlighting their journeys, strategies, and the impressive success they have achieved.

Through these case studies, we will explore the diverse ways digital real estate can be leveraged to build wealth and create impactful online presences.

Individuals and their Digital Real Estate Exploits

Emma Johnson: The Blog Queen of Sustainable Living

Emma Johnson, from Portland, Oregon, turned her passion for sustainability into a digital empire. In 2012, she started a blog called "EcoLover," focusing on eco-friendly lifestyle tips, DIY projects, and sustainable product reviews. Emma's unique voice and dedication to high-quality content quickly attracted a loyal readership.

Strategies and Success:

- **Content Creation:** Emma's consistent and valuable content, paired with effective SEO strategies, boosted her blog's visibility.

- **Affiliate Marketing:** Partnering with eco-friendly brands, Emma monetized her blog through affiliate links, earning commissions on products her readers purchased.

- **Advertising:** She utilized Google AdSense and direct advertising deals with green companies.

By 2020, "EcoLover" was generating over $100,000 annually, with traffic exceeding 500,000 visitors per month. Emma's blog not only provided a steady income but also positioned her as an influencer in the sustainability niche.

Mark Thompson: The Domain Name Mogul

Mark Thompson, an entrepreneur from London, saw potential in domain names early on. He began his journey by buying undervalued domain names and selling them at a profit, a practice known as domain flipping.

Strategies and Success:

- **Research:** Mark meticulously researched market trends, identifying domain names that would appreciate in value.

- **Portfolio Diversification:** He built a diverse portfolio of domains, covering various industries and niches.

- **Sales Channels:** Mark utilized platforms like Sedo and Flippa to buy and sell domains.

One of his notable successes was the sale of "TravelGuru.com" for $500,000, which he had purchased for just $10,000. Over a decade, Mark's domain flipping business amassed a net worth of over $5 million, making him a renowned figure in the digital real estate world.

Aisha Khan: The Social Media Maven

Aisha Khan, from Dubai, recognized the power of social media early in her career. She started with an Instagram account focused on luxury travel, @LuxTraveler, sharing breathtaking travel photos and experiences.

Strategies and Success:

- **Engaging Content:** Aisha's high-quality visuals and engaging captions attracted a large following.

- **Brand Collaborations:** She partnered with luxury hotels and travel brands for sponsored posts.

- **Account Sales:** Seeing the demand for well-established social media accounts, Aisha began buying and selling Instagram accounts.

Within five years, @LuxTraveler grew to over a million followers. Aisha's social media ventures not only generated substantial income from sponsorships and advertisements but also led to lucrative sales of multiple Instagram accounts, each valued at over $100,000.

Raj Patel: The E-commerce Pioneer

Raj Patel, an enterprising businessman from Mumbai, capitalized on the e-commerce boom. He founded an online store, "TechGuru.in," specializing in affordable tech gadgets and accessories.

Strategies and Success:

- **Product Sourcing:** Raj sourced products directly from manufacturers, ensuring competitive pricing.

- **Digital Marketing:** He invested in SEO, Google Ads, and social media marketing to drive traffic to his store.

- **Customer Service:** Superior customer service and fast shipping built a loyal customer base.

"TechGuru.in" grew rapidly, reaching an annual revenue of $2 million within three years. Raj's success in e-commerce allowed him to expand into other niches, establishing a network of profitable online stores.

Maria Fernandez: The App Developer Extraordinaire

Maria Fernandez, a software engineer from Barcelona, turned her coding skills into a lucrative business by developing mobile apps. She founded "SmartApps Co.," creating utility and productivity apps for smartphones.

Strategies and Success:

- **User-Centric Design:** Maria focused on creating user-friendly apps that solved everyday problems.

- **Freemium Model:** Her apps were free to download, with premium features available through in-app purchases.

- **App Store Optimization:** She used effective ASO techniques to ensure her apps ranked high in app stores.

One of her most successful apps, "TaskMaster," a task management app, garnered over 10 million downloads and generated $1 million in revenue from in-app purchases and ads. Maria's portfolio of apps brought her company to a valuation of $10 million.

Ethan and Olivia Zhang: Virtual Real Estate Investors

Ethan and Olivia Zhang, a visionary couple from Beijing, ventured into the emerging field of virtual real estate. They invested in digital properties within popular virtual worlds like Decentraland and The Sandbox.

Strategies and Success:

- **Early Adoption:** They were among the first to see the potential of virtual real estate and made early investments.

- **Development:** They developed virtual storefronts, art galleries, and event spaces, attracting virtual foot traffic.

- **Monetization:** Their virtual properties generated income through virtual rent, advertising, and hosting virtual events.

Their investment portfolio grew exponentially, with virtual properties worth over $3 million. The Zhangs became pioneers in a new frontier of digital real estate, blending innovation with investment acumen.

Mark Zuckerberg: The Social Network Titan

Mark Zuckerberg, co-founder and CEO of Facebook (now Meta), transformed the concept of social networking. What started as a college project at Harvard University turned into one of the world's most influential digital real estate platforms.

Strategies and Success:

- **User Engagement:** Facebook's success hinged on its ability to keep users engaged and connected.

- **Advertising:** Zuckerberg leveraged Facebook's massive user base to create a powerful advertising platform, generating billions in revenue.

- **Acquisitions:** Strategic acquisitions like Instagram and WhatsApp expanded Meta's digital real estate footprint.

Today, Meta's platforms are used by over 3 billion people globally, and the company's market cap exceeds $900 billion, showcasing the immense value of social media as digital real estate.

Jeff Bezos: The E-commerce Emperor

Jeff Bezos, founder of Amazon, revolutionized the digital economy through his innovative approach to e-commerce. What began as an online bookstore in 1994 grew into the largest online retailer in the world.

Strategies and Success:

- **Customer Focus:** Amazon's success is built on its unwavering focus on customer satisfaction and convenience.

- **Diversification:** Bezos expanded Amazon's offerings to include everything from cloud computing (AWS) to streaming services (Prime Video).

- **Innovation:** Continuous innovation, including advancements in logistics and AI, kept Amazon ahead of competitors.

Amazon's market cap now exceeds $1.5 trillion, and Bezos' vision has made him one of the richest individuals in the world, underscoring the power of digital real estate in e-commerce.

Peter Thiel: The Venture Capital Visionary

Peter Thiel, co-founder of PayPal and early investor in Facebook, has a keen eye for identifying and nurturing digital real estate opportunities. His venture capital firm, Founders Fund, has backed numerous successful digital ventures.

Strategies and Success:

- **Early Investment:** Thiel's early investment in Facebook turned a $500,000 stake into billions of dollars.

- **Diverse Portfolio:** His investments span various sectors, including fintech (Stripe), biotech (Palantir), and space exploration (SpaceX).

- **Disruptive Innovation:** Thiel focuses on companies that have the potential to disrupt traditional industries and create new digital markets.

Thiel's strategic investments have not only yielded substantial financial returns but also shaped the landscape of the digital economy, demonstrating the critical role of venture capital in digital real estate.

The Global Impact of Digital Real Estate

These stories from around the world illustrate the diverse opportunities within digital real estate. From blogs and domain names to social media accounts, e-commerce stores, mobile apps, and virtual properties, the potential for success is vast. These entrepreneurs harnessed their unique skills, innovative ideas, and strategic thinking to build substantial wealth and influence in the digital realm.

Their journeys highlight the importance of identifying trends, investing wisely, and continuously adapting to the ever-evolving digital landscape. As the world becomes increasingly digital, the opportunities for building and investing in digital real estate will only continue to grow, promising exciting futures for those willing to take the plunge.

One of the most effective ways to learn about digital real estate is through the experiences of those who have successfully navigated this dynamic landscape. In this chapter, we will delve into real-world examples by presenting interviews with successful digital real estate entrepreneurs and analyzing some of the most successful digital properties. These case studies will provide valuable insights and lessons that can be applied to your own digital ventures.

Interviews with Successful Digital Real Estate Entrepreneurs

Interview 1: John Smith, Founder of TechSavvyBlog

John Smith, the founder of TechSavvyBlog, started his journey in digital real estate in 2012. Today, his blog attracts millions of visitors monthly and generates substantial revenue through advertising, affiliate marketing, and digital product sales.

- **Background**: John began TechSavvyBlog as a hobby, sharing his passion for technology and gadgets. Over time, his consistent, high-quality content started attracting a significant audience.

- **Key Strategies**:
  - **Niche Focus**: John emphasized the importance of focusing on a specific niche. By targeting tech enthusiasts, he was able to build a loyal and engaged audience.

- ○ **SEO Mastery**: Investing time in learning SEO techniques paid off. He optimized his content for search engines, leading to increased organic traffic.

  ○ **Monetization Mix**: Diversifying income streams through ads, affiliate marketing, and selling digital products like e-books and courses helped stabilize his revenue.

- **Lessons Learned**:

  ○ **Patience and Consistency**: Building a successful digital property takes time and consistent effort. John advises new bloggers to stay patient and persistent.

  ○ **Community Engagement**: Actively engaging with readers through comments, social media, and email newsletters helped build a strong community around his blog.

Interview 2: Jane Doe, E-commerce Entrepreneur and Owner of TrendyFashionStore

Jane Doe is a successful e-commerce entrepreneur who built TrendyFashionStore, a thriving online boutique specializing in sustainable fashion.

- **Background**: Jane launched TrendyFashionStore in 2016 with a mission to promote eco-friendly fashion. Today, her store is a leading name in the niche.

- **Key Strategies**:
    - **Brand Identity**: Jane focused on creating a strong brand identity centered around sustainability. This resonated with a growing segment of eco-conscious consumers.
    - **Social Media Marketing**: Leveraging platforms like Instagram and Pinterest, Jane built a substantial following. Her visually appealing posts and influencer collaborations drove significant traffic to her store.
    - **Customer Experience**: Offering exceptional customer service and a seamless shopping experience helped retain customers and encouraged word-of-mouth referrals.
- **Lessons Learned**:
    - **Market Research**: Understanding market trends and customer preferences is crucial. Jane continuously monitors industry developments to stay ahead.
    - **Adaptability**: Being adaptable and willing to pivot based on feedback and market changes is key to long-term success.

Analyzing Successful Digital Properties

What Makes Them Successful?

Case Study 1: SmartPassiveIncome.com by Pat Flynn

SmartPassiveIncome.com, created by Pat Flynn, is a leading resource for entrepreneurs looking to generate passive income online. The site offers a wealth of information, including blogs, podcasts, and online courses.

- **Key Factors of Success**:
    - **Transparency**: Pat Flynn's transparent approach, sharing his income reports and personal experiences, built trust with his audience.
    - **Value-Driven Content**: Offering high-value content for free established Pat as an authority in the passive income space.
    - **Diverse Revenue Streams**: SmartPassiveIncome.com generates income through affiliate marketing, online courses, sponsorships, and more.
- **Key Takeaways**:
    - **Authenticity**: Being genuine and transparent can significantly enhance credibility and trust.

- Educational Content: Providing valuable, educational content attracts and retains a dedicated audience.

Case Study 2: The Points Guy (TPG)

The Points Guy (TPG) is a renowned travel website that helps readers maximize their travel rewards and loyalty points. Founded by Brian Kelly, TPG has become a go-to resource for travelers.

- Key Factors of Success:
    - Expertise: Brian Kelly's expertise and passion for travel rewards are evident in the detailed guides and reviews on TPG.
    - Engaging Content: The site features a mix of blog posts, videos, and interactive tools, keeping the content engaging and accessible.
    - Partnerships: Strategic partnerships with airlines, hotels, and credit card companies have enhanced TPG's offerings and revenue streams.
- Key Takeaways:
    - Niche Expertise: Deep knowledge and expertise in a specific niche can differentiate a site and build a loyal following.

- **Multimedia Approach**: Using various content formats can cater to different audience preferences and enhance engagement.

General Key Takeaways

1. **Niche Focus**: Successful digital properties often target specific niches. Focusing on a well-defined niche helps in building a dedicated and engaged audience.

2. **High-Quality Content**: Providing valuable, high-quality content consistently is crucial. This not only attracts visitors but also encourages repeat visits and builds authority.

3. **Diverse Monetization Strategies**: Relying on multiple income streams, such as advertising, affiliate marketing, and digital products, can stabilize and increase revenue.

4. **Audience Engagement**: Actively engaging with your audience through comments, social media, and email newsletters fosters community and loyalty.

5. **SEO and Marketing**: Effective SEO practices and robust marketing strategies, including social media and email marketing, are vital for driving traffic and growing digital properties.

6. **Adaptability and Innovation**: Staying adaptable and continuously innovating based on market

trends and feedback ensures long-term relevance and success.

By studying these case studies and success stories, you can gain valuable insights and practical strategies to apply to your own digital real estate ventures. Whether you are just starting out or looking to scale your existing digital property, these lessons from successful entrepreneurs and properties will guide you on your journey to success.

Chapter 8: LEGAL AND FINANCIAL CONSIDERATIONS

Navigating the legal and financial aspects of digital real estate is crucial for the long-term success and sustainability of your digital ventures. This chapter explores the key legal and financial considerations, from protecting your intellectual property to managing your finances and understanding tax implications.

Legal Aspects of Digital Real Estate

Intellectual Property Rights

Intellectual property (IP) rights are essential for protecting the unique content and branding of your digital property. Understanding and securing these rights can prevent unauthorized use and ensure you maintain control over your digital assets.

1. **Copyrights**: Copyright law protects original works of authorship, such as blog posts, images, videos, and software. As the creator, you automatically own the copyright to your work upon creation. To enhance protection:

    o **Register Your Work**: Registering your work with the relevant authorities you r country can provide additional legal benefits and make it easier to enforce your rights.

    o **Use Copyright Notices**: Displaying a copyright notice on your digital property can deter infringement and inform others of your ownership.

2. **Trademarks**: Trademarks protect brand elements such as logos, slogans, and names that distinguish your products or services from those of others.

    o **Registration**: Registering your trademark with the appropriate government agency (e.g., the USPTO in the United States) provides legal protection and helps prevent others from using similar marks.

    o **Monitoring and Enforcement**: Regularly monitor the use of your trademarks and take legal action if necessary to prevent unauthorized use.

3. **Patents**: If you develop a unique process, system, or technology, you may be able to protect

it with a patent. This is more relevant for software and innovative digital products.

- **Patent Application**: The patent application process can be complex and requires detailed documentation of your invention. Consulting with a patent attorney is advisable.

Privacy Policies and Terms of Service

Privacy policies and terms of service (TOS) are legal agreements that help protect your digital property and inform users of their rights and responsibilities.

1. **Privacy Policies**: A privacy policy outlines how you collect, use, and protect users' personal information. It is legally required in many jurisdictions and builds trust with your audience.

    - **Key Elements**: Include information about data collection methods, types of data collected, purposes of data use, data sharing practices, and user rights.

    - **Compliance**: Ensure your privacy policy complies with relevant regulations, such as the General Data Protection Regulation (GDPR) in the European Union or the California Consumer Privacy Act (CCPA) in the United States and the Federal Consumer Protection Commission in Nigeria.

2. **Terms of Service**: The TOS agreement sets the rules for using your website or digital service. It can help limit your liability and set clear expectations for users.

    - **Content Ownership**: Specify who owns the content and what users can and cannot do with it.

    - **User Conduct**: Outline acceptable and prohibited behaviors, such as spamming or hacking.

    - **Dispute Resolution**: Include a clause on how disputes will be handled, whether through arbitration, mediation, or court proceedings.

Financial Management

Budgeting and Investment Strategies

Effective financial management is critical for the growth and sustainability of your digital real estate. This involves budgeting, investing, and managing cash flow.

1. **Budgeting**: Creating a budget helps you plan and control your expenses, ensuring that you allocate resources efficiently.

    - **Income and Expenses**: Track all sources of income and categorize expenses (e.g., hosting fees, marketing, software subscriptions).

- **Forecasting**: Estimate future revenue and expenses to plan for growth and anticipate financial challenges.

2. **Investment Strategies**: Investing wisely in your digital property can lead to substantial growth and returns.

    - **Reinvestment**: Reinvest a portion of your profits back into your business to fund marketing campaigns, software upgrades, or hiring additional staff.

    - **Diversification**: Diversify your investments by exploring different revenue streams or expanding into new digital properties.

3. **Cash Flow Management**: Maintaining a healthy cash flow is essential for covering operational costs and investing in growth opportunities.

    - **Accounts Receivable and Payable**: Monitor your receivables and payables to ensure timely payments and collections.

    - **Emergency Fund**: Maintain an emergency fund to cover unexpected expenses or downturns in revenue.

Tax Considerations for Digital Entrepreneurs

Understanding and managing your tax obligations is crucial for avoiding legal issues and optimizing your financial health.

1. **Business Structure**: Your business structure (sole proprietorship, LLC, corporation) affects your tax obligations and liability.

    o **Sole Proprietorship**: Simple to set up, but you are personally liable for business debts and taxes.

    o **LLC**: Offers liability protection and flexible tax options. Profits and losses can pass through to your personal tax return.

    o **Corporation**: Provides strong liability protection but involves more complex tax filings and regulations.

2. **Tax Deductions**: Digital entrepreneurs can take advantage of various tax deductions to reduce taxable income.

    o **Business Expenses**: Deduct ordinary and necessary business expenses, such as hosting fees, software subscriptions, marketing costs, and office supplies.

    o **Home Office**: If you work from home, you may be eligible for a home office deduction, which allows you to deduct a portion of your home expenses related to your business.

3. **Sales Tax**: If you sell digital products or services, you may be required to collect sales tax depending on your location and where your customers are based.

- **Nexus Rules**: Understand the nexus rules in different jurisdictions, as they determine where you need to collect sales tax.

- **Compliance**: Use tools like TaxJar or Avalara to help manage and automate sales tax collection and remittance.

4. **Estimated Taxes**: As a digital entrepreneur, you may need to pay estimated taxes quarterly to avoid penalties.

    - **Calculation**: Estimate your tax liability based on expected income and make timely payments to the IRS or your local tax authority.

    - **Record Keeping**: Keep detailed records of all income and expenses to accurately calculate your tax liability and support your tax filings.

In conclusion, managing the legal and financial aspects of digital real estate is vital for protecting your assets, ensuring compliance, and optimizing financial performance. By understanding intellectual property rights, crafting clear privacy policies and terms of service, implementing effective budgeting and investment strategies, and staying on top of your tax obligations, you can create a solid foundation for the growth and sustainability of your digital ventures.

Chapter 8: TRENDS AND FUTURE OF DIGITAL REAL ESTATE

The landscape of digital real estate is constantly evolving, driven by technological advancements and changing consumer behaviors. This chapter explores emerging trends in digital real estate, including the influence of AI and blockchain, and offers predictions for the future.

Emerging Trends in Digital Real Estate

AI and Automation

Artificial Intelligence (AI) and automation technologies are revolutionizing how digital real estate is managed and monetized.

1. **Personalization and User Experience:**

- AI-powered algorithms analyze user behavior and preferences to deliver personalized content and recommendations. According to a report by Gartner, organizations that incorporate AI into their personalization strategies can increase profitability by up to 15%.

2. **Chatbots and Customer Support**:
   - Chatbots use AI to provide instant responses to customer queries, improving user engagement and satisfaction. Research by IBM indicates that businesses can reduce customer service costs by up to 30% by implementing AI-powered chatbots.

3. **Content Generation**:
   - AI algorithms can generate content based on data inputs, reducing the time and resources required for content creation. Tools like OpenAI's GPT-3 have been used to generate blog posts, product descriptions, and social media content.

4. **Predictive Analytics**:
   - AI-driven predictive analytics forecast market trends and user behavior patterns, enabling digital real estate entrepreneurs to make informed decisions and optimize strategies in real-time.

Blockchain and Cryptocurrency in Digital Real Estate

Blockchain technology and cryptocurrencies are increasingly being integrated into digital real estate transactions and ownership models.

1. **Smart Contracts**:
   - Smart contracts, powered by blockchain technology, facilitate secure and transparent transactions without the need for intermediaries. They automate contract execution based on predefined conditions, reducing costs and improving efficiency.

2. **Tokenization of Assets**:
   - Real estate assets are being tokenized, allowing investors to buy and trade fractional ownership units. This democratizes access to real estate investments and enhances liquidity in the market.

3. **Decentralized Finance (DeFi)**:
   - DeFi platforms leverage blockchain to offer decentralized lending, borrowing, and liquidity pooling services. These platforms enable real estate crowdfunding and investment opportunities outside traditional banking systems.

4. **Property Records and Transparency:**
    - Blockchain enables secure storage of property records, reducing fraud and ensuring transparency in real estate transactions. According to a Deloitte survey, 55% of real estate professionals believe blockchain will be widely adopted within five years.

Predictions for the Future

What to Expect in the Next 5-10 Years

1. **Augmented Reality (AR) and Virtual Reality (VR):**
    - AR and VR technologies will transform property viewing experiences, allowing potential buyers to virtually tour homes and properties from anywhere in the world. This immersive experience enhances decision-making and reduces the need for physical visits.

2. **Sustainable and Green Real Estate:**
    - There will be a growing emphasis on sustainable and eco-friendly real estate developments. Green buildings and renewable energy with digital solutions will become standard features, driven by environmental concerns and regulatory incentives.

3. **Global Market Expansion**:

    o Digital platforms and blockchain technologies will facilitate cross-border real estate transactions, expanding investment opportunities globally. Investors can diversify portfolios with international properties more easily.

4. **Integration of Big Data and IoT**:

    o Big data analytics and Internet of Things (IoT) devices will provide real-time insights into property performance, maintenance needs, and tenant behavior. This data-driven approach will optimize property management and enhance operational efficiency.

Preparing for Future Trends

1. **Investment in Technology**:

    o Stay updated with technological advancements in AI, blockchain, AR/VR, and IoT. Investing in these technologies can give you a competitive edge and improve operational efficiency.

2. **Adaptability and Flexibility**:

    o Remain agile and adaptable to changes in consumer preferences and market dynamics. Embrace new trends and adjust strategies accordingly to capitalize on emerging opportunities.

3. **Regulatory Awareness**:
   - Monitor regulatory developments related to blockchain, cryptocurrencies, and data privacy. Compliance with evolving regulations will be crucial to mitigate legal risks and maintain trust with stakeholders.

4. **Continuous Learning and Skill Development**:
   - Develop skills in data analytics, digital marketing, and emerging technologies. Continuous learning will equip you to leverage future trends effectively and innovate within the digital real estate space.

In conclusion, the future of digital real estate promises exciting opportunities driven by AI, blockchain, and emerging technologies. By embracing these trends, preparing for future developments, and maintaining a proactive approach to innovation, digital real estate entrepreneurs can position themselves for sustained growth and success in the years to come.

Chapter 10: TOOLS AND RESOURCES FOR DIGITAL REAL ESTATE

Effective management and growth of digital real estate require leveraging the right tools and staying informed through valuable resources.

This chapter explores essential tools for managing digital assets and recommends reading and learning resources to enhance your expertise in the field.

Essential Tools for Managing Digital Assets

Website Builders and Hosting Services

1. **Website Builders**:
    - **WordPress**: A versatile platform with a vast ecosystem of plugins and themes. WordPress powers a significant portion of

the internet due to its flexibility and scalability.

- **Wix**: Offers intuitive drag-and-drop features for easy website building without coding skills. Ideal for beginners and small businesses.

- **Shopify**: Specifically designed for e-commerce, Shopify provides robust tools for setting up and managing online stores.

2. **Hosting Services**:

    - **Bluehost**: Known for its reliability and affordability, Bluehost offers hosting plans optimized for WordPress websites.

    - **SiteGround**: Offers excellent customer support and performance-enhancing features like free CDN and daily backups.

    - **Amazon Web Services (AWS)**: Ideal for scalable solutions, AWS provides cloud hosting services suitable for high-traffic websites and applications.

SEO Tools and Analytics Platforms

1. **SEO Tools**:

    - **Google Analytics**: Provides comprehensive insights into website traffic, user behavior, and conversion rates. It's free and widely used.

- **SEMrush**: Offers competitive analysis, keyword research, and SEO auditing tools to optimize your website's search engine performance.

- **Ahrefs**: Known for its backlink analysis and site audit capabilities, Ahrefs helps improve your website's authority and ranking.

2. **Analytics Platforms**:

    - **Google Search Console**: Monitors and optimizes your website's presence in Google search results. It provides data on search queries, indexing status, and more.

    - **Hotjar**: Offers heatmaps, session recordings, and user feedback tools to understand how visitors interact with your website and identify optimization opportunities.

    - **Mixpanel**: Focuses on user behavior analytics, helping you track user actions and improve user experience across your digital properties.

Recommended Reading and Learning Resources

Books, Blogs, and Online Courses

1. **Books:**
   - *SEO 2024: Learn Search Engine Optimization with Smart Internet Marketing Strategies* by Adam Clarke. This book covers up-to-date SEO techniques and strategies.
   - *The Lean Startup* by Eric Ries. Although not specific to digital real estate, it offers valuable insights into building successful businesses through iterative testing and learning.
   - *Blockchain Revolution* by Don Tapscott and Alex Tapscott. Explores the potential impact of blockchain technology on various industries, including real estate.

2. **Blogs and Online Resources:**
   - **Moz Blog**: Offers in-depth articles on SEO, digital marketing trends, and best practices.
   - **HubSpot Blog**: Covers a wide range of topics, including inbound marketing, sales, and customer service strategies.
   - **Neil Patel's Blog**: Provides actionable insights on SEO, content marketing, and

digital strategy from industry expert Neil Patel.

3. **Online Courses and Webinars**:
    - **Coursera**: Offers courses on digital marketing, SEO fundamentals, and web development from universities and industry experts.
    - **Udemy**: Provides a wide range of courses on WordPress, e-commerce, SEO, and digital entrepreneurship.
    - **HubSpot Academy**: Offers free certification courses on inbound marketing, content marketing, and social media strategy.

Industry Experts and Influencers to Follow

1. **Neil Patel (@neilpatel)**:
    - Digital marketing expert known for his insights on SEO, content marketing, and entrepreneurship.

2. **Rand Fishkin (@randfish)**:
    - Co-founder of Moz and a leading authority on SEO and inbound marketing.

3. **Brian Dean (@Backlinko)**:

- Founder of Backlinko, offering practical SEO advice and strategies for improving search rankings.

4. **Gary Vaynerchuk (@garyvee):**
    - Entrepreneur and digital marketing expert known for his insights on social media marketing and business growth strategies.

By utilizing the essential tools discussed in this chapter and tapping into recommended reading and learning resources, you can equip yourself with the knowledge and tools necessary to effectively manage and grow your digital real estate.

Staying updated with industry trends and learning from established experts will empower you to optimize your digital assets, drive traffic, and maximize revenue opportunities in the competitive digital landscape.

Chapter 11: COMMUNITY AND NETWORKING

Building a strong community and networking effectively are essential strategies for success in digital real estate. This chapter explores how to cultivate a community around your digital assets and capitalize on networking opportunities within the industry.

Building a Community Around Your Digital Real Estate

Engaging with Your Audience

1. **Content Quality and Consistency:**
    - Deliver high-quality content that addresses the needs and interests of your target audience. Consistency in posting helps maintain engagement and build trust.

- Encourage interaction through comments, polls, and discussions to foster a sense of community and gather valuable feedback.

2. **Social Media Engagement**:
    - Utilize platforms like Instagram, Facebook, Twitter, and LinkedIn to connect with your audience. Share content regularly and engage with followers through likes, shares, and direct messaging.
    - Create groups or communities within social media platforms where members can share experiences, ask questions, and support each other.

3. **Email Newsletters and Updates**:
    - Build an email list and send regular newsletters with curated content, updates, and exclusive offers. Personalize emails to enhance engagement and encourage interaction.

4. **Live Q&A Sessions and Webinars**:
    - Host live sessions where you interact directly with your audience, answer their questions, and provide valuable insights. Webinars on relevant topics can establish authority and attract new followers.

Creating a Supportive Network

1. **Partnering with Influencers and Collaborators**:

    o Collaborate with influencers or industry experts to reach a wider audience and gain credibility. Joint ventures or co-hosted webinars can leverage each other's strengths and resources.

    o Participate in guest blogging opportunities or podcast interviews to introduce your digital property to new audiences.

2. **Building Relationships with Subscribers and Customers**:

    o Focus on building long-term relationships with your subscribers and customers. Offer personalized support, respond promptly to inquiries, and address concerns professionally.

    o Implement loyalty programs or exclusive membership benefits to reward repeat customers and encourage brand advocacy.

Networking Opportunities

Digital Real Estate Forums and Groups

1. **Online Forums and Communities:**
   - Join digital real estate forums such as Reddit's r/realestateinvesting or BiggerPockets to network with like-minded individuals, share experiences, and learn from others' successes and challenges. You can join my real estate forum and collaborators @digitalrealestatepro.com
   - Participate actively by contributing valuable insights, asking questions, and offering support to establish yourself as a knowledgeable and respected member.

2. **LinkedIn Groups and Facebook Communities:**
   - LinkedIn groups focused on digital marketing, SEO, and entrepreneurship can connect you with professionals in the industry. Engage in discussions and connect with members who share similar interests or goals.
   - Facebook communities for digital entrepreneurs, bloggers, or e-commerce enthusiasts provide opportunities for networking, collaboration, and knowledge sharing.

Attending Conferences and Webinars

1. **Industry Conferences and Events**:

   - Attend digital marketing conferences, SEO summits, and real estate expos to network with industry leaders, discover emerging trends, and gain valuable insights.

   - Participate in workshops, panel discussions, and networking sessions to expand your knowledge and connect with potential partners or clients.

2. **Webinars and Virtual Events**:

   - Participate in webinars hosted by industry experts or organizations relevant to digital real estate. These events offer opportunities to learn new strategies, ask questions, and interact with speakers and attendees.

   - Virtual networking events allow you to connect with professionals from around the world, build relationships, and explore potential collaborations or joint ventures.

Effective community building and networking are integral to maximizing the potential of your digital real estate ventures. By engaging with your audience through valuable content, social media interactions, and live sessions, you can cultivate a loyal community that supports and advocates for your brand.

Additionally, actively participating in online forums, industry groups, and attending conferences or webinars will expand your professional network, foster collaborations, and keep you informed about industry trends and opportunities.

Embrace these strategies to strengthen your digital presence, establish meaningful connections, and accelerate the growth of your digital real estate portfolio.

Chapter 12: RECAP OF KEY THEMES

Digital real estate remains a dynamic and rapidly evolving sector within the broader digital economy. Throughout this book, we have explored various facets of digital real estate, from its definition and historical evolution to practical strategies for acquisition, monetization, management, and growth.

1. **Definition and Importance of Digital Real Estate**:
    - o Digital real estate encompasses a diverse range of digital assets, including websites, domain names, social media accounts, e-commerce stores, mobile apps, and virtual properties. These assets hold intrinsic value and can be leveraged for financial gain, brand building, and audience engagement.

2. **Historical Evolution**:
    - From the early days of the internet to the present, digital properties have grown exponentially in significance. What started as simple websites has expanded into complex ecosystems involving advanced technologies like AI, blockchain, and virtual reality.

3. **Getting Started with Digital Real Estate**:
    - The journey begins with identifying your niche, conducting thorough market research, and leveraging your passion and expertise to acquire digital assets. Valuation and due diligence are crucial steps in ensuring the viability and potential return on investment of these assets.

4. **Monetization Strategies**:
    - Various monetization avenues exist for digital real estate, including affiliate marketing, advertising through platforms like Google AdSense, selling digital products such as e-books and courses, and implementing subscription models. Each strategy requires careful planning and execution to maximize revenue.

5. **Management and Growth**:
   - Effective content creation, SEO practices, social media marketing, email marketing, and analytics play pivotal roles in managing and growing digital properties. These activities not only drive traffic and engagement but also optimize user experience and conversion rates.

6. **Legal and Financial Considerations**:
   - Managing intellectual property rights, drafting robust privacy policies and terms of service, and navigating financial aspects such as budgeting, investment strategies, and tax considerations are essential for mitigating risks and ensuring compliance in the digital realm.

7. **Emerging Trends and Future Predictions**:
   - AI and automation, blockchain technology, augmented reality (AR), and virtual reality (VR) are poised to revolutionize digital real estate. Looking ahead, sustainable practices, global market expansion, and advancements in data analytics and IoT will shape the future landscape.

8. **Tools, Resources, and Community Building**:
   - Leveraging essential tools like website builders, SEO platforms, and analytics

tools enhances operational efficiency and performance. Meanwhile, continuous learning through books, blogs, online courses, and networking with industry experts and communities fosters innovation and professional growth.

Embracing the Future of Digital Real Estate

As digital real estate continues to evolve, entrepreneurs and investors must remain agile, adaptable, and proactive in embracing emerging technologies and market trends. By staying informed, leveraging cutting-edge tools, nurturing a supportive community, and actively networking, individuals can position themselves for sustained success in this dynamic industry.

Digital real estate offers unparalleled opportunities for creativity, innovation, and profitability. Whether you're a seasoned entrepreneur or just starting your journey, the principles and strategies outlined in this book provide a solid foundation for navigating the complexities and harnessing the potential of digital assets.

The future of digital real estate is bright and full of possibilities. By applying the insights and strategies discussed, you can embark on a journey of growth, resilience, and continuous evolution in the ever-expanding digital landscape.

CHAPTER 13: CONCLUSION

Building digital real estate or investing in digital real estate and the digital economy is becoming increasingly compelling as the world continues to shift towards digital platforms for commerce, communication, and entertainment. Here's why you should consider this lucrative and future-oriented investment:

Compelling Statistics

1. **Market Growth**: The global digital economy was valued at over $11.5 trillion in 2020 and is projected to grow at a compound annual growth rate (CAGR) of 15% through 2025.

2. **E-commerce Boom**: E-commerce sales reached $4.28 trillion globally in 2020, with projections to hit $6.39 trillion by 2024.

3. **Online Content Consumption**: More than 4.66 billion people use the internet as of 2021, and

digital content consumption is growing exponentially, with video streaming alone expected to account for 82% of all internet traffic by 2022.

4. **Social Media Influence**: Over 3.78 billion people were using social media worldwide in 2021, with an annual growth rate of 5.1%. This widespread usage opens up enormous potential for monetizing digital assets like social media accounts and online communities.

Success Stories and New Entrant

1. **Jeff Bezos and Amazon**: Jeff Bezos founded Amazon in his garage in 1994, initially as an online bookstore. Today, Amazon is the world's largest online retailer, with a market cap of over $1.7 trillion. Bezos's foresight in digital commerce has made him one of the richest individuals in the world.

2. **Mark Zuckerberg and Facebook**: Mark Zuckerberg created Facebook in 2004, which has grown into a social media giant with over 2.8 billion monthly active users. The platform's advertising revenue reached $84.2 billion in 2020, demonstrating the immense monetization potential of social media.

3. **Peter Thiel and PayPal**: Peter Thiel co-founded PayPal, which revolutionized online payments. The company was sold to eBay for $1.5 billion in 2002. Thiel's early investment in Facebook also

yielded significant returns, exemplifying successful digital real estate investment.

4. **Pat Flynn and Smart Passive Income**: Pat Flynn is an entrepreneur who turned his blog into a multi-million dollar business. His website, Smart Passive Income, generates income through affiliate marketing, advertising, and digital products, showcasing the potential of monetizing online content.

5. **Michelle Schroeder-Gardner and Making Sense of Cents**: Michelle Schroeder-Gardner started a personal finance blog that now earns over $100,000 per month through affiliate marketing, sponsored posts, and digital products. Her success story highlights the profitability of niche websites.

6. **TikTok**: Launched in 2016, TikTok has quickly become one of the most valuable digital properties, now worth over $100 billion. The platform's explosive growth and widespread adoption, particularly among younger demographics, underscore the vast potential of investing in innovative digital platforms.

7. **Ijigban Daniel Oketa**: focused on mind renovation and safety, I am developing H-TIPS into a user App and online platform for global adoption by billions of people with the potential to transform humanity and the world into more peaceful place in unity of mind and purpose.

Advantages of Investing in Digital Real Estate

1. **Low Entry Barrier**: Starting an online business or investing in digital assets often requires lower capital compared to traditional real estate.

2. **Scalability**: Digital businesses can reach a global audience without the limitations of physical location, allowing for rapid scalability.

3. **Passive Income**: Many digital real estate investments, such as websites and online stores, can generate passive income through advertising, affiliate marketing, and automated sales.

4. **High ROI**: With the right strategies, digital real estate can yield higher returns on investment compared to traditional investments. For example, domain flipping, where domains are bought at low prices and sold at higher values, can result in significant profits.

Investing in digital real estate and the digital economy offers unparalleled opportunities for growth and profitability. As more of the world's economy moves online, the potential for high returns continues to expand. By leveraging digital platforms, understanding market trends, and learning from successful entrepreneurs, you can position yourself to benefit from this dynamic and rapidly evolving landscape.

About the Book

Discover the transformative power of digital assets and seize the opportunity to participate in the digital real estate market to create generational wealth. This book empowers you with a comprehensive understanding of digital real estate and the global digital economy, covering all essential aspects, including:

1. The difference between digital real estate and digital economy.
2. How to start, launch or invest in the highly profitable global real estate and digital economy.
3. Monetizing, managing and growing your digital real estate.
4. Case studies and success stories of various investments in digital real estate.
5. Legal and financial considerations of digital real estate.
6. Trends and future of digital real estate.
7. Tools and resources for digital real estate.

Ideas are not just the new oil; to make the most of your ideas, you need to create digital real estate for them. Investing in the global digital economy is key to creating unlimited passive income and achieving wealth creation.

This book provides the knowledge and tools to turn your ideas into profitable digital assets, enabling you to build a sustainable and prosperous future.

The Author

Over the past decade, I have established myself as a versatile adviser, coach, teacher, and consultant, working across numerous industries. My expertise in human capital, business development, and investment consulting has allowed me to collaborate with a wide array of organizations, groups, and individuals worldwide.

My journey is a testament to resilience and growth, demonstrating how the creation and implementation of H-TIPS (Human and Time Innovation Power System) have revolutionized personal development, transformative leadership, and societal change.

I am also the host of "Humanity About All Things" (HAAT) @haatglobal, where I explore and discuss topics that matter to humanity.

Follow me on social media @idoketa to stay connected and inspired.

Contact me for Collaboration and Partnership

+234 703-738-4814
oketadaniels@gmail.com

www.ingramcontent.com/pod-product-compliance
Lightning Source LLC
Chambersburg PA
CBHW071939210526
45479CB00002B/749